BEARCUB BIOS

HUMANITARIAN

by Rachel Rose

Consultant: Beth Gambro
Reading Specialist, Yorkville, Illinois

Minneapolis, Minnesota

Teaching Tips

BEFORE READING

- Discuss what a biography is. What kinds of things might a biography tell a reader?
- Look through the glossary together. Read and discuss the words.
- Go on a picture walk, looking through the pictures to discuss vocabulary and make predictions about the text.

DURING READING

- Encourage readers to point to each word as it is read. Stop occasionally to ask readers to point to a specific word in the text.
- If a reader encounters an unknown word, ask them to look at the rest of the page. Are there any clues to help them understand?

AFTER READING

- Check for understanding.
  - Where was Meghan Markle born?
  - What does she do?
  - What does she care about?
- Ask the readers to think deeper.
  - If you met Meghan, what question would you like to ask her? Why?

Credits:
Cover, © Geoffrey Robinson/Alamy Stock Photo; Title page, © Geoffrey Robinson/Alamy Stock Photo; 3, © Alan Fraser Images/Shutterstock; 5, © WPA Pool/Getty Images; 7, © STEVE PARSONS/Getty Images; 8, © Charley Gallay/Getty Images; 11, © addkm/Shutterstock; 13, © Bryan Pollard/Alamy Stock Photo; 14-15, © USA Network/Getty Images; 16, © dpa picture alliance/Alamy Stock Photo; 19, © WPA Pool/Getty Images; 20-21, © lev radin/Shutterstock; 22, © Kathy Hutchins/Shutterstock; 23TL, © nicoletaionescu/iStock; 23TR, © michaeljung/Shutterstock; 23BL, © SbytovaMN/iStock; and 23BR, © kiwiofmischief/Shutterstock.

Library of Congress Cataloging-in-Publication Data

Names: Rose, Rachel, 1968– author. Title: Meghan Markle : Humanitarian / by Rachel Rose. Description: Minneapolis, Minnesota: Bearport Publishing Company, [2021] | Series: Bearcub bios | Includes bibliographical references and index. Identifiers: LCCN 2020000151 (print) | LCCN 2020000152 (ebook) | ISBN 9781642809794 (library binding) | ISBN 9781642809909 (paperback) | ISBN 9781647470012 (ebook) Subjects: LCSH: Meghan, Duchess of Sussex, 1981–Juvenile literature. | Princesses—Great Britain—Biography—Juvenile literature. | Women philanthropists—Great Britain—Biography—Juvenile literature. | Television actors and actresses—United States—Biography—Juvenile literature. Classification: LCC DA591.A45 M4476 2021 (print) | LCC DA591.A45 (ebook) | DDC 941.086092 [B]—dc23 LC record available at https://lccn.loc.gov/2020000151LC ebook record available at https://lccn.loc.gov/2020000152

Copyright © 2021 Bearport Publishing Company. All rights reserved. No part of this publication may be reproduced in whole or in part, stored in any retrieval system, or transmitted in any form or by any means, electronic, mechanical, photocopying, recording, or otherwise, without written permission from the publisher.

For more information, write to Bearport Publishing, 5357 Penn Avenue South, Minneapolis, MN 55419.

Printed in the United States of America.

Contents

A Royal Day.................... 4
Meghan's Life.................. 6

Did You Know?........................... 22
Glossary 23
Index 24
Read More 24
Learn More Online....................... 24
About the Author 24

A Royal Day

It was a big day for Meghan Markle.

She married Prince Harry of England.

Meghan was very happy.

Meghan's Life

Meghan was born in California.

Her mother is African American, and her father is white.

Meghan is proud of that fact.

Growing up, Meghan wanted to be an **actor**.

Her father worked on TV shows.

One day, she got to be on one of his shows!

Meghan also cared about people.

She helped people who didn't have food.

She wanted the same **rights** for men and women.

Meghan went to **college**.

She did acting.

She also learned about working with people around the world.

After college, she got some small acting jobs.

Meghan went to school here.

In 2011, Meghan got a big **part** in a TV show.

The woman she played was named Rachel.

Rachel was smart and strong.

So is Meghan.

Meghan playing Rachel

Meghan was busy.

But she still helped others.

She went to the country of Rwanda.

She helped people get clean water.

Meghan met Prince Harry in 2016.

They got married.

Then, they had a son named Archie.

Meghan and her family moved away from England.

They still help others.

Meghan will always be a star no matter where she lives.

Did You Know?

Born: August 4, 1981

Family: Doria (mother), Thomas (father)

When she was a kid: Her mom gave her the nickname Flower.

Special fact: Meghan's full name is Rachel Meghan Markle. She has the same first name as Rachel from her TV show!

Meghan says: "Be grateful for the little things."

Life Connections

Meghan likes to help people. What things do you like to do? Can some of those things help others?

Glossary

actor a person who acts on stage, on TV, or in the movies

college school that people go to after high school

part the role of a character in a play or show

rights basic things that everyone should have or be able to do

Index

acting 9, 12
California 6
England 4, 21
Prince Harry 4–5, 18
rights 10
Rwanda 17
TV shows 9, 14, 22

Read More

Golkar, Golriz. *Meghan Markle (Influential People).* North Mankato, MN: Capstone Press (2019).

McDaniel, Sarita. *Princesses (Meet the Royals).* New York: Enslow (2019).

Learn More Online

1. Go to **www.factsurfer.com**
2. Enter "**Meghan Markle**" into the search box.
3. Click on the cover of this book to see a list of websites.

About the Author

Rachel Rose lives in San Francisco with her husband and her dog, Sandy. Sandy is the biggest star she knows.